CHESTER CATHEDRAL

Contents
Visitors' Guide	opposite
The Benedictine Abbey	2
The Nave	8
The Choir	13
The Carvings	14
The Chapels	17
The Cathedral Today	19

Above:
Aerial view of the cathedral, showing the 13th-century refectory and cloisters, the precincts and the bell tower.

Left:
The Moses panel, a detail from the mosaic panels on the north wall of the nave.

The Benedictine Abbey

The story of Chester Cathedral begins in 907 with the fortification of Chester by Ethelfleda, the martial sister of Edward the Elder, King of Wessex, as a strongpoint against the half-heathen Norse from Ireland who were settling in Wirral. Soon after 907 a church was founded on the site of the present cathedral. In the church were placed the relics of St. Werburgh, brought from Hanbury in Staffordshire. St. Werburgh, who had died between 700 and 707, was the daughter of Wulfhere, king of Mercia. Like a great many other royal ladies of her time she became a nun and was placed by her father in charge of all the convents in Mercia. Up until 1092 the church of St. Werburgh was a minster staffed by a college of twelve clergymen, called canons, under a *custos*, or warden. Each had his own house near the church. They were responsible for the daily services and guarded the relics of St. Werburgh, and they were also parish priests, as St. Werburgh's was the parish church of an area embracing most of Chester and extending a good way into Wirral. Nothing is left of the Anglo-Saxon minster except two filled-in doorways in the south-east corner of the cloister.

In the reign of William Rufus, in 1092, Hugh Lupus, the second earl of Chester, wanted to turn St. Werburgh's into an abbey of Benedictine monks. His great friend, St. Anselm, the abbot of Bec in Normandy came to Chester in September 1092 to advise him how to do it. At the time of his visit he was beginning to plan the greatest of his writings, that on the meaning of the Death of Christ, *Cur Deus Homo*.

From 1092 to 1540 the present cathedral was a Benedictine abbey in the diocese of Lichfield. The first abbot and monks came from Bec. In the course of the 12th and 13th centuries the Anglo-Saxon church was replaced by the first abbey church which stretched from the present west end to just short of the present high altar.

The first abbey church had two transepts, each with an apsidal chapel on the east side. The arch and triforium in the east wall of the present north transept belonged to the north transept of the first abbey church. They date from the end of the 11th century and are the oldest part of the cathedral.

Between 1250 and 1538 the first abbey church was gradually replaced by the church we see today. To the early 14th century belongs the base of St. Werburgh's Shrine which since 1889 has stood at the west end of the Lady

Right: (20)
The cloisters, laid out in the 12th century, were largely rebuilt 1525–37 and restored by Giles Scott 1911–13.

Below: (14)
The Shrine of St. Werburgh, c.1310, where up to 6 people at a time could put in their heads and confess their sins. In 1540 the saint's bones were moved to safety by the monks and have not been found.

Chapel. On it would have been placed the chest containing her relics. No reliable evidence is available as to where the Shrine stood in the Middle Ages.

The south transept up to triforium level was built in the middle years of the 14th century. Its size, out of all proportion to the north transept, was determined by the need for providing altars. The monastic buildings on the north side of the church made an extension of the north transept impossible. Instead, an extra large south transept was built. At the same time the rebuilding of the nave was begun with the south arcade, similar in design to the arcades of the south transept. The last great building period in the Middle Ages was from 1484 to 1537. To these years belong the north arcade of the nave, the clerestory windows, the south-west corner of the nave where the consistory court is, the south-west porch, the west front and the top stage of the central tower.

The abbey inherited the parochial responsibilities of the Anglo-Saxon minster. The parishioners used the south aisle of the nave as their parish church, which was dedicated to St. Oswald. When the rebuilding of the nave began in the mid-14th century they moved out to a guild chapel dedicated to St. Nicholas, the remains of which can be seen in St. Werburgh Street opposite the south-west porch. In the early decades of the 16th century they were given the south transept as their parish church. It was called St. Oswald's and remained their parish church till 1881, a partition at the north end separating it from the rest of the cathedral. The same arrangement is found in Spanish cathedrals which have a parish. The parishioners worship in an area – often the *sagrario* – which though structurally belonging to the cathedral is cut off from the parts used for the cathedral services and has its own outside entrance.

Some evidence is available of the number of monks belonging to the abbey. In the middle of the 13th century there were about forty, towards the end of the 14th century about thirty, and when the abbey was dissolved in 1538 there were at least twenty-eight. The main work of the monks was the singing of the divine office in choir day by day. The magnificent choir stalls, about 1390 in date, bear witness to the importance placed on this work of worship. Incidentally, the choir was divided from the nave by a stone screen, and part of it can be seen in the north choir aisle at the back of the stalls. Although St. Anselm,

Above:
The north transept. The oldest part of the cathedral is the late 11th-century round arch and arcade above it. Beyond the arch is the Sacristy made in 1930 out of a 13th-century chapel. Here the vestments are kept.

Left:
The baptistery, which was made in 1885 in the north-west corner of the early 12th-century nave. The font, given in 1885, came from Venice.

who presided over the abbey's foundation, was one of the greatest thinkers of all time, the monks were not distinguished for their intellectual gifts until the 14th century when the abbey produced the great popular historian of the later Middle Ages, Ranulph Higden.

At the suggestion of his brother monks he wrote a history of the world beginning at the Creation and brought his narrative down to 1352. It is called the *Polychronicon*. Higden's narrative has been described as scrappy and repetitive; but it contains some lively character sketches. He died in 1364 and was buried in the south choir aisle just east of the blocked-up door. The grave was opened in 1874. His bones were in a stone coffin, and wrapped in a coarse woollen cloth of reddish brown; they dissolved directly they were touched. But the 14th-century abbey also produced the earliest of the Chester Mystery Plays. The plays, of which twenty-four are extant, deal with the Christian scheme of salvation from the Creation to the Last Judgement. According to a Chester tradition of 1532, they were 'devised and made' by a Henry Francis, who is among the monks signing documents dealing with the abbey between 1377 and 1382. He may have been the author of the earliest plays, but many were written in the 15th century. Since 1951 there have been regular peformances in Chester of the plays, the abbey's great contribution to the story of English drama.

Chester Cathedral is fortunate in possessing many of the buildings where the monks lived. They are among the best preserved monastic buildings in Great Britain and give a far better idea of a medieval abbey than the celebrated Cistercian ruins in Yorkshire. They are on the north side of the cathedral, built round the cloister, which was originally laid out when the first abbey church was built in the 12th century. To the 12th-century cloister belong the two doorways into the cathedral from the south cloister and the blind arches along its wall, and the undercroft leading off the west wall. This was the monks' cellar and is now the cathedral workshop.

The other buildings are later in date. Off the east cloister is the chapter house where the monks met each day in conference, preceded by its beautiful vestibule and their parlour. These are of 13th-century date. Over them was the monks' dormitory, which has been destroyed. It had two staircases – one used by the monks in the daytime, just by the door to the parlour, and the other leading from the dormitory to the north transept, by which they came down to the choir for the night office. Along the

Right: [20]
The refectory with the cloister garden, laid out in the 1920s, in the foreground. From the early 17th century until 1876 the refectory was used by the King's School, founded as part of the cathedral in 1541.

Below: [20]
The refectory was the monks' dining hall. The pulpit on the right was for a monk to read from during meals. The abbot and his chief guests sat on the stone dais at the end. St. Werburgh and her relations are depicted in the 20th-century east window.

north cloister is one of the most noble medieval rooms in existence, the monks' dining hall. It, too, is of 13th-century date; but with 15th-century windows in the side walls, which fill it with light. The cloisters, the windows, stone vaults and the carrels in the south cloisters where the monks did their reading and illuminating, were built between 1525 and 1538 in the very last days of the abbey. The entrance to the monastic buildings from the city was through Abbey Gate, which led into the outer courtyard of the abbey, now Abbey Square. Round the courtyard were various buildings used in the abbey's administration, for instance store-rooms and the brew house. On the south side of the courtyard and joined to the south-west corner of the nave was the abbot's lodging, St. Anselm's Chapel being his private chapel.

On 20 January 1540, the abbey came to an end with its surrender to the Crown; on 26 July 1541, the former abbey church was made the cathedral of the newly formed diocese of Chester. The church received a new dedication: Christ and the Blessed Virgin Mary; and was in future to be staffed by a dean and chapter of six prebendaries (canons) with six minor canons, six lay clerks and eight choristers for singing the services. The first prebendaries were either former monks or friars; the last abbot became the first dean. Today the cathedral clergy consist of the dean, three canons, and one chaplain choral who corresponds to the former minor canons.

Below:
The 13th-century refectory doorway was the main doorway used by monks from the cloisters to the refectory. Beyond is the monks' washplace.

The Nave

The history of the cathedral since 1541 falls into two well-defined periods: 1541–1868; and 1868 to the present day. Owing to the restorations carried out since 1868, very little distinctive work of the 17th, 18th or early 19th centuries remains. In 1600 the flagged floor of the nave was laid, though it has been repaired several times since. The bishop of Chester in the time of Charles I, John Bridgeman, took a great interest in the cathedral. He generously provided the oak furnishings of the consistory court and the screen that separates it from the nave, and the screen, altar rails and plaster ceiling in St. Anselm's Chapel. He also probably gave the great tapestry which now hangs in the refectory. In the south-west corner of the nave is a font, given in 1687. Apart from monuments, such as the Wainwright monument by Berkeley and Kent, the Peploe monument by Nollekens, and two delicate monuments by Richard Hayward, the cathedral has little to show from the 18th century. In 1819 the chapter called in the Chester architect Thomas Harrison to advise them about the fabric; and the present south front of the south transept was rebuilt according to his design.

In the 1840s the revived interest in medieval architecture and church furnishings began to make itself felt in the cathedral. Considerable alterations were carried out in the choir from 1843–6. The arch between the choir and the Lady Chapel was opened up; and the familiar vista through the choir to the east end of the Lady Chapel created. The choir was rearranged by the architect R. C. Hussey. The stonework of the east window (1846) over the high altar is his work; so also are the balustrades in the choir triforium and the nave pulpit. In 1855 he built the doorway and windows between the chapter house vestibule and the east cloister. From 1850 onwards a number of stained-glass windows were placed in the cathedral.

In the north-west corner of the nave, near the font, are the arches, dating from about 1140, of what was intended to be the north-west tower of this church. The choir and each of its aisles ended in an apse; these are marked in the floor of the present north and south choir aisles. The bases of two of the columns of the choir can be seen in the north choir aisle against the back of the choir stalls.

Right:
The nave, looking east.

Below:
One of four 1883–6 mosaic panels portraying Old Testament scenes.

Bottom:
In 1636 the ground floor of the south-west tower became the consistory court, the only surviving one in England.

The main part of the organ, rebuilt in 1969, stands in the archway between the tower crossing and the north transept. The loft and case (1876) were designed by Gilbert Scott.

A detail from the choir screen, designed in 1876 by Gilbert Scott, which divided the choir from the nave.

The Choir

Left: ⑪
In the choir stalls the daily services of Mattins and Evensong are sung by the cathedral clergy and choir.

Below: ⑬
The High Altar. The mosaic reredos (1876) is by Salviati.

The church we see today began with the Lady Chapel c.1250–75 and then the choir, which was finished in the early years of the 14th century. The architect of the choir was Richard of Chester, one of the military engineers responsible for Edward I's castles in North Wales.

Since 1868 the whole appearance of the cathedral, inside and out, has been altered by a series of restorations. Of these, much the greatest was that of the nave, choir, Lady Chapel and exterior carried out from 1868–76 by Gilbert Scott, who added many new features. The credit for much of the work belongs to James Frater, Scott's clerk of works; and in the north choir aisle is a brass to his memory. The present arrangement of the interior of the cathedral is due to Scott. He replaced the stone screen between the nave and choir by the open wooden screen. It makes the sanctuary the focal point of worship from the nave, enhances the sense of space, and gives the cathedral an atmosphere of reverence and prayer. Between the tower crossing and the north transept the organ loft and case were built, forming a splendid terminus to the vista from the south transept. The present arrangement of the choir and the stalls also dates from Scott's restoration. Particularly fine is the brown tile floor, which tones with the sandstone.

The sanctuary was planned by J. S. Howson, the greatest of the Victorian deans of Chester. In the floor are two Clayton representations of the Passover, surrounded by pieces of tessellated pavement from the temple area at Jerusalem. The wood of the altar table is from the Holy Land. Prophets by J. R. Clayton look down from the ceiling. Thus the sanctuary symbolises the earthly Jerusalem, where the Lord's death and passion, foretold by the Old Testament, was accomplished. But over the altar is the mosaic of the Last Supper, where Our Lord instituted the Holy Communion as 'a perpetual memory' of His death and passion. At the Holy Communion He gives us the heavenly food of His Body and Blood. So the sanctuary symbolises the heavenly Jerusalem, where 'God feeds His Israel for ever with the food of truth, and life is the wisdom by whom all things are made' (Augustine).

The Carvings

Above:
The reredos in St. Oswald's Chapel was designed by C. E. Kempe and carved in Oberammagau.

Left:
The most popular of all symbols of the medieval church, the pelican in her piety, restoring her young to life by blood from her own breast – carved on the end of the Vice-Dean's stall.

Right:
Elephant and castle bench end, showing the medieval carver's lack of familiarity with elephants!

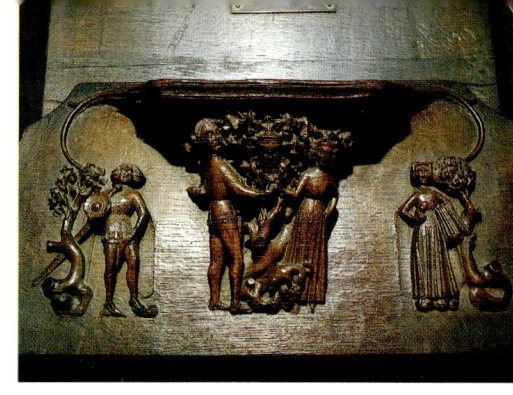

Left:
This fox in friar's robe receives a blessing while the gullible folk he will swindle await him among the trees.

Top right:
Tristram and Iseult meet under a tree beneath which the deceived husband shelters.

Left:
The St. Werburgh legend – the slain goose is restored; the culprit, detected, confesses.

Right:
The end of the Dean's Stall, previously the Abbot's Stall. On it is a Tree of Jesse surmounted by the coronation of Our Lady. On the elbow rest is a pilgrim to the shrine of St. Werburgh.

Misericords were small ledges on the undersides of tip-up seats in the choir stalls, to support monks during long services. Medieval carvers lavished great wit and social comment on these rarely seen places; 43 survive at Chester, 3 of which are shown here.

Below:
The Wainwright memorial, c.1722, by the west door, is a unique signed work of George Berkeley, Anglican philosopher and future Bishop of Cloyne, and the great architect William Kent. It commemorates John Wainwright and his son Thomas, successive chancellors of the diocese of Chester.

Left:
A lion bench end; there are 36 bench ends of which almost half are 14th century.

Right:
The Annunciation, carved on a spandrel of a bench end.

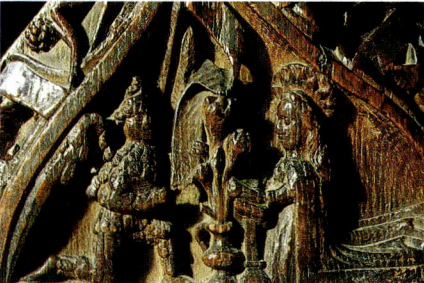

15

The Chapels

Left: ⑭
In 1960 the Lady Chapel was redecorated by Bernard Miller and the lampshades designed by his partner, Duncan M. Stewart. It was built 1250–75 and brought back to its original form by Gilbert Scott in 1868–73. The glass is by Wailes: in the east window are the Passion and Resurrection: in the side windows are scenes from the lives of SS. Peter and Paul. The altar frontal (1965) in blue and gold was designed by George Pace.

Right: ⑩
The Chapel of St. Erasmus is in the south choir aisle and is set apart for private prayers. Here the Blessed Sacrament is reserved. The stained glass windows represent Faith, Hope, Charity and Humility.

At the end of 1881 the south transept ceased to be used by St. Oswald's as their parish church. In 1882 Sir Arthur Bloomfield restored the east aisle and in 1887 placed the great window in the south wall, with its stained-glass *The Triumph of Faith*, by Heaton, Butler and Bayne. The rest of the interior of the transept was restored 1900–2 by Charles James Bloomfield. A striking feature of the transept are the four altars in a row in the east aisle. In the first bay

from the south is the St. Nicholas altar (1917) and in the second the St. George altar (1921). Both were designed by Giles Scott. In the third bay is the St. Oswald altar (1906) by Kempe, and the stained glass in the windows over these altars is by him. The last altar, St. Mary Magdalene (1922), is by Tower. The bay with the St. George altar is the chapel of the Cheshire Regiment. Along the east wall are the regimental colours, including those in which the coffin of Wolfe was wrapped after the Battle of Quebec (1759). In the bay in the west aisle opposite St. George's chapel is the cenotaph (1933) designed by Giles Scott with the Regimental Book of Remembrance of the First World War. The Book of Remembrance of the Second World War is in the case nearby. In the window (1949) near the south-west door is the *Risen and Glorified Christ* by H. M. Doyle.

Between 1911 and 1914 the monastic buildings were restored by Giles Scott. The east, north and west cloisters are his work as is also the east window of the refectory. In the monastic buildings the cathedral has a magnificent plant for playing its part as a cathedral in the modern world. Their possibilities were first realised by Dean Bennet (1920–37).

Under his imaginative leadership they were once more used as an integral part of the cathedral's day-to-day life. The parlour and refectory became rooms which could be used for meetings, visiting parties and diocesan gatherings. A kitchen was made in 1923 at the west end of the refectory so that meals can be served. The cloisters became a place to walk in sheltered from the elements, and a garden was laid out in the middle. The work of bringing the monastic buildings into modern use was completed in 1939 with the building of F. H. Crossley's magnificent hammerbeam in the refectory.

Above:
The finely carved oak reredos and French marble altar frontal of St. George's Chapel (since 1912 the chapel of the Cheshire Regiment) were designed in 1921 by Sir Giles Scott, when the chapel, originally dedicated to St. Leonard, was re-dedicated to St. George.

Left:
Thomas Green, Mayor of Chester in 1565, is shown on his memorial flanked by both his wives. The hands of all three have been broken off, possibly by Puritans who objected to hands in a position of prayer. Thomas died without issue and willed his money to be 'employed in good and charitable uses'.

The Cathedral Today

The restorations were carried out by two firms, John Thompson and Son of Peterborough, and William Haswell and Son of Chester, and are a lasting monument to the excellence of their craftsmen. Since 1946, under the direction of Bernard Miller, the main roofs have been covered with copper and in the aisle roofs timber has been replaced with metal. In 1961 came one of the greatest treasures, the west window of the nave by W. T. Carter Shapland, with its tall hieratic figures, and in 1966 George Pace's exciting nave stalls.

A feature of the 19th-century restorations were the rib-vaulted ceilings. Until the 1840s all parts of the cathedral except the Lady Chapel had open timber roofs. Hussey, 1844–6, put a rib-vaulted ceiling with lathe and plaster in-filling over the choir under the timber roof. Gilbert Scott removed Hussey's ceiling and placed the oak rib-vaulted ceilings over the nave and choir; and C. J. Blomfield put a similar ceiling over the south transept. Of recent years emphasis has been laid on the importance of the principle 'partiality' in gothic architecture. The principle springs from the use of rib-vaulting, whether of wood or of stone. A characteristic of a medieval rib-vaulted church is that each part is a fragment of the whole. This characteristic is more than an architectural feature. It makes a church speak a great Christian truth. Chester Cathedral too, with its 19th-century rib-vaulted ceilings, is able to speak that truth:

Man is but a fragment of creation. He finds his totality by taking his place in the Kingdom of God.

Above:
The Victorian heaters, made by Gurney's Patent Warming & Ventilating Co., were originally coke-heated, converted to oil, and then gas.

Below:
An Edward I cupboard, in the Chapter House.

Top left:
An important modern addition to the complex of the cathedral buildings is the free-standing Bell Tower, or Campanile, opened in 1975 and designed by George Pace. There is a ring of twelve bells and a flat $\frac{1}{6}$th, re-cast from nine of the ten bells that, until 1969, hung in the central tower of the cathedral.

Left:
Cheshire Youth Choir and Regimental Band of the Prince of Wales' Own Regiment of Yorkshire performing at a 'Carolcade' for the National Children's Homes.

The west window showing the Virgin and Child with 6 northern saints.